GRADE 3 PHONICS:
Name And Say That Object

BABY PROFESSOR

EDUCATION KIDS

Speedy Publishing LLC
40 E. Main St. #1156
Newark, DE 19711
www.speedypublishing.com

PHONICS

A method of teaching people to read and pronounce words by learning the sounds of the letters, letter groups, and syllables.

BOOK

\\'bu̇k\\

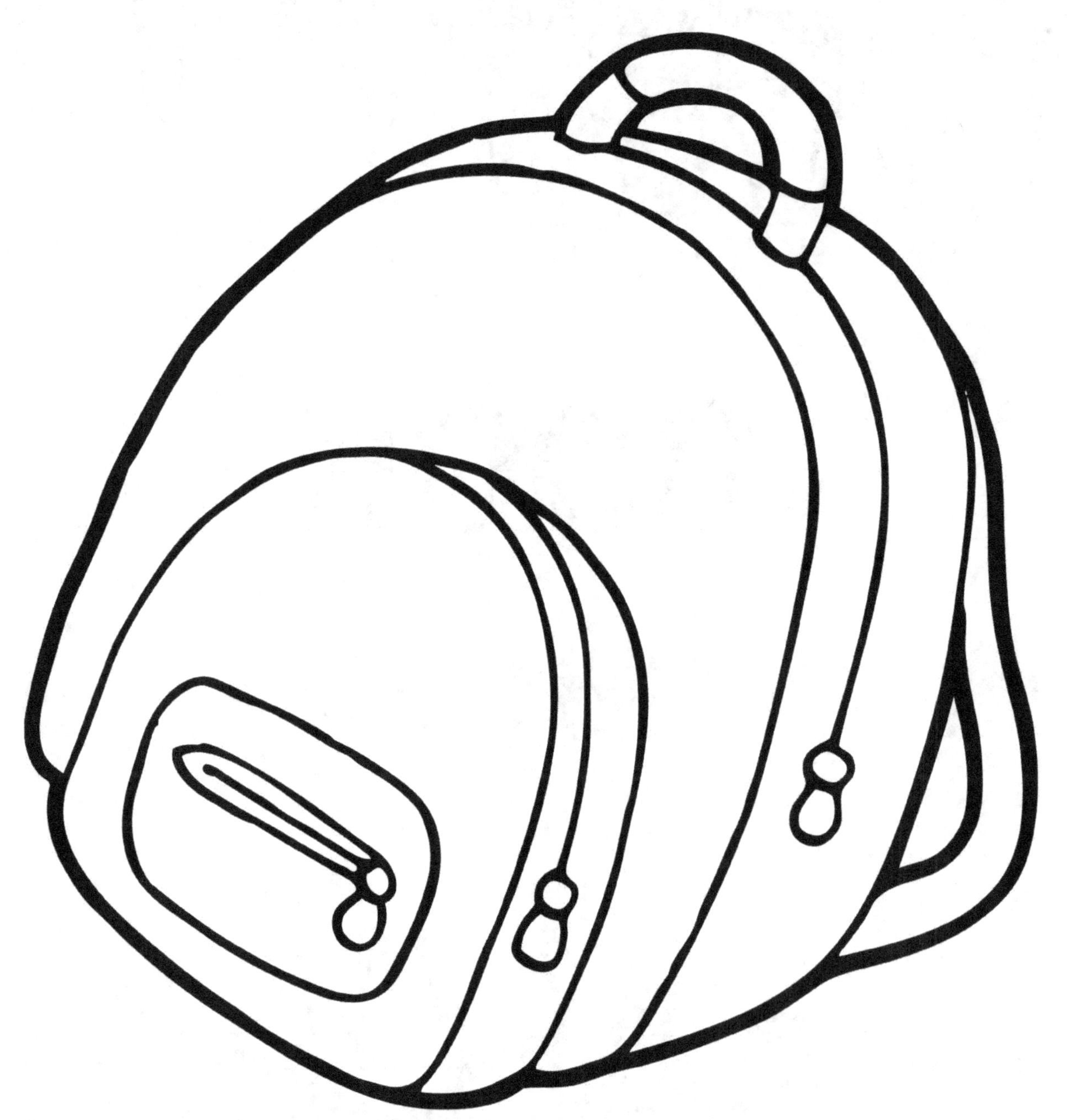

BAG

\\ˈbag, ˈbāg\\

TRACTOR

\\'trak-tər\\

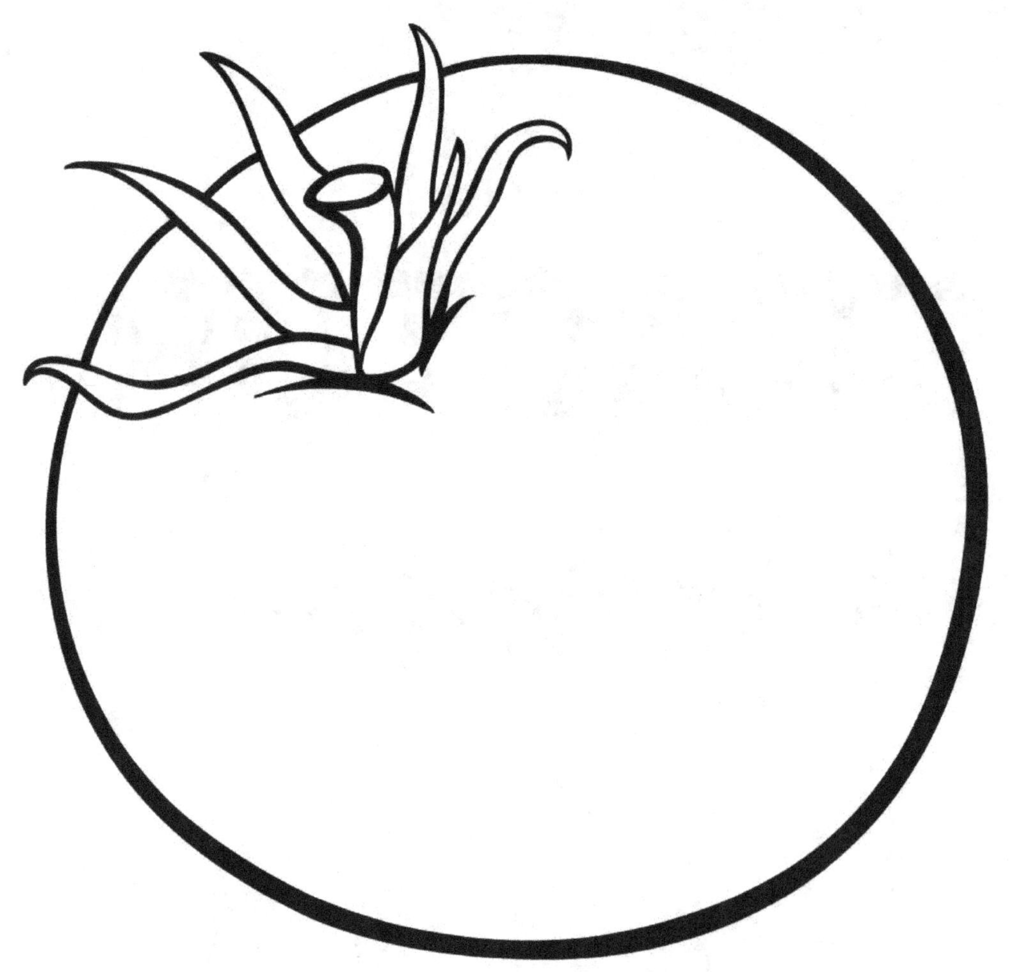

TOMATO

\tə-ˈmā-(ˌ)tō\

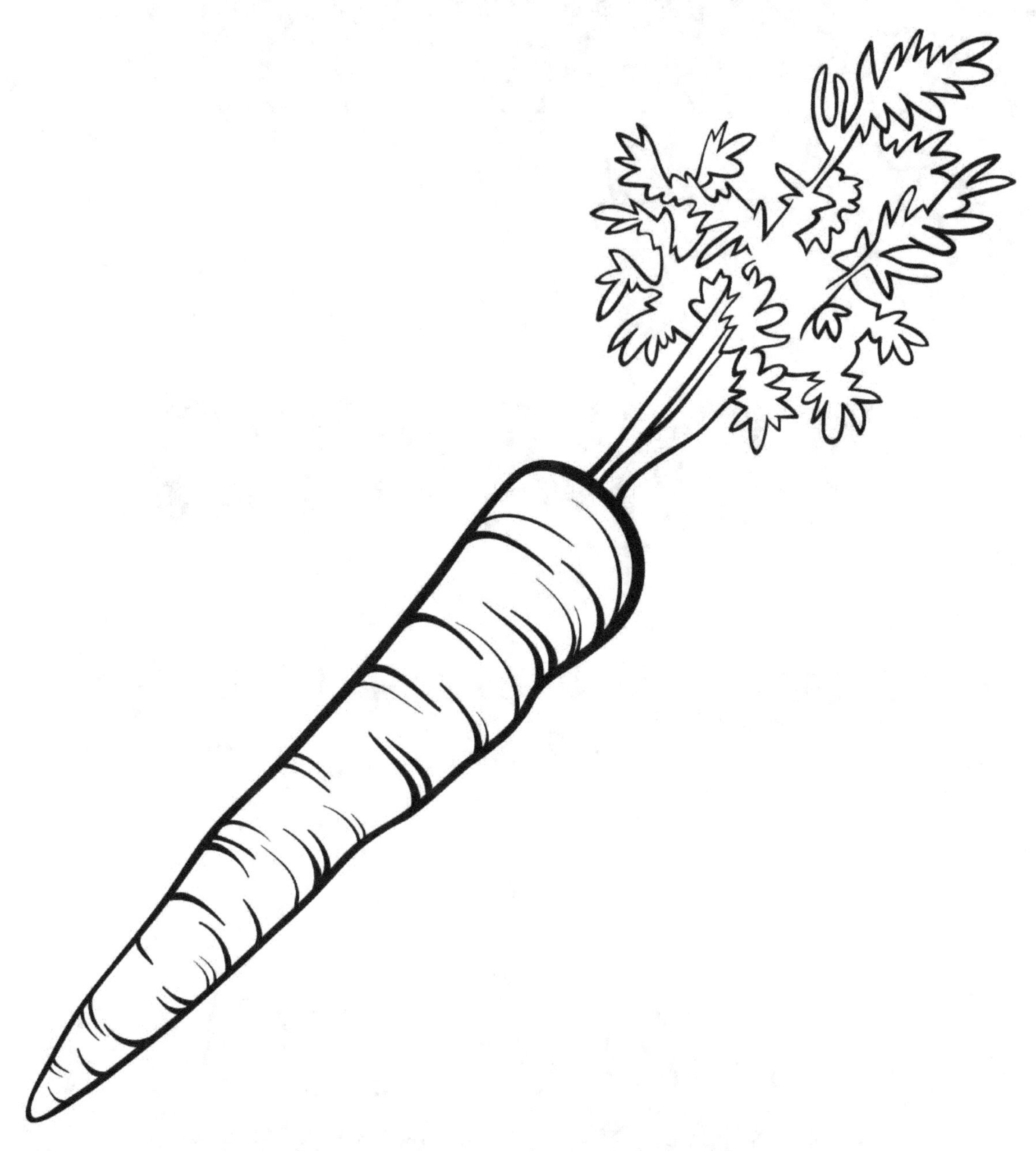

CARROT

\ˈker-ət, ˈka-rət\

PENCIL

\ˈpen(t)-səl\

BROCCOLI

\ˈbrä-kə-lē, ˈbrä-klē\

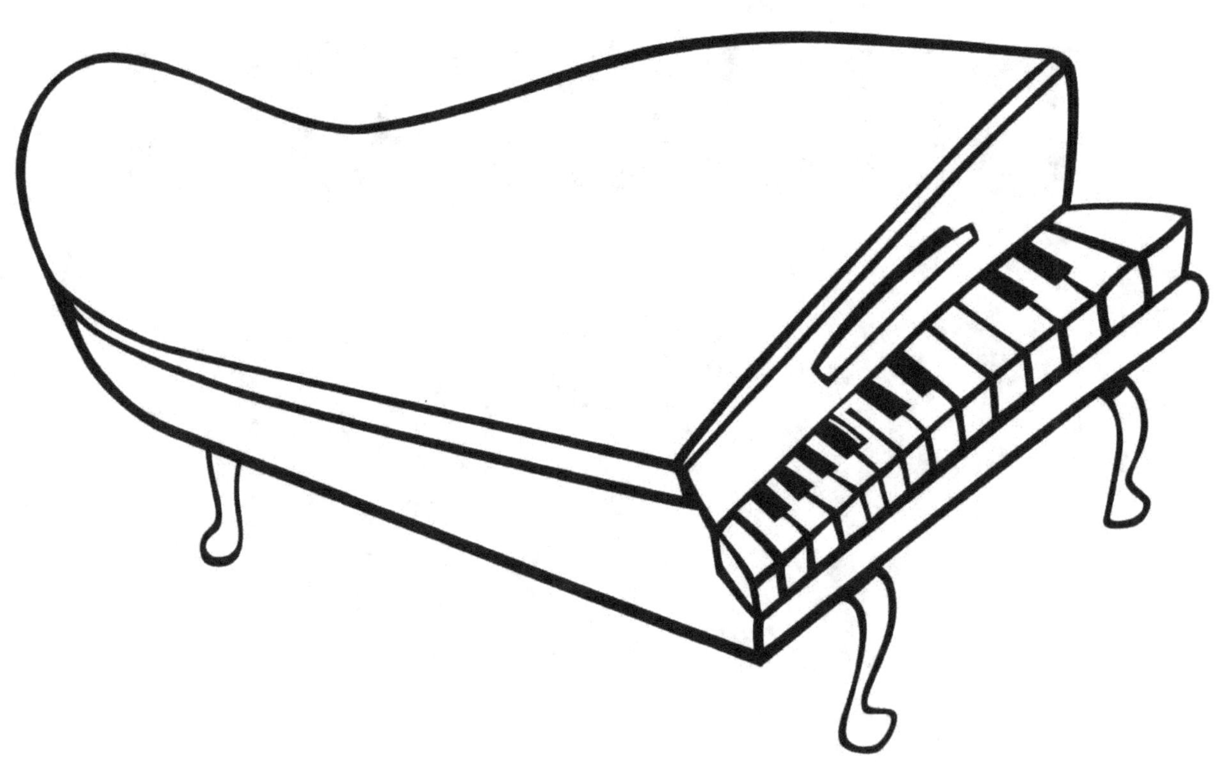

PIANO

\pē-ˈä-(ˌ)nō\

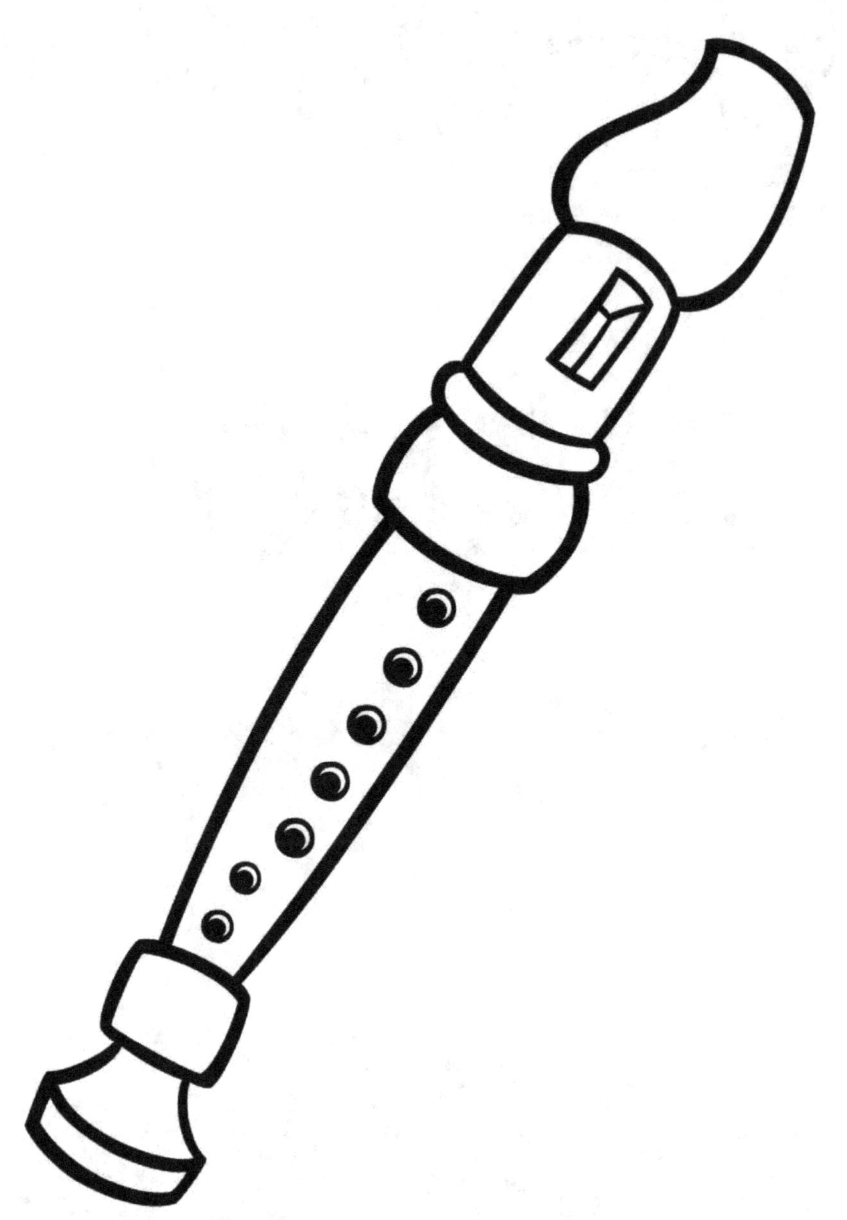

FLUTE

\ˈflüt\

DRUM

\\'drəm\\

GUITAR

\gə-ˈtär\

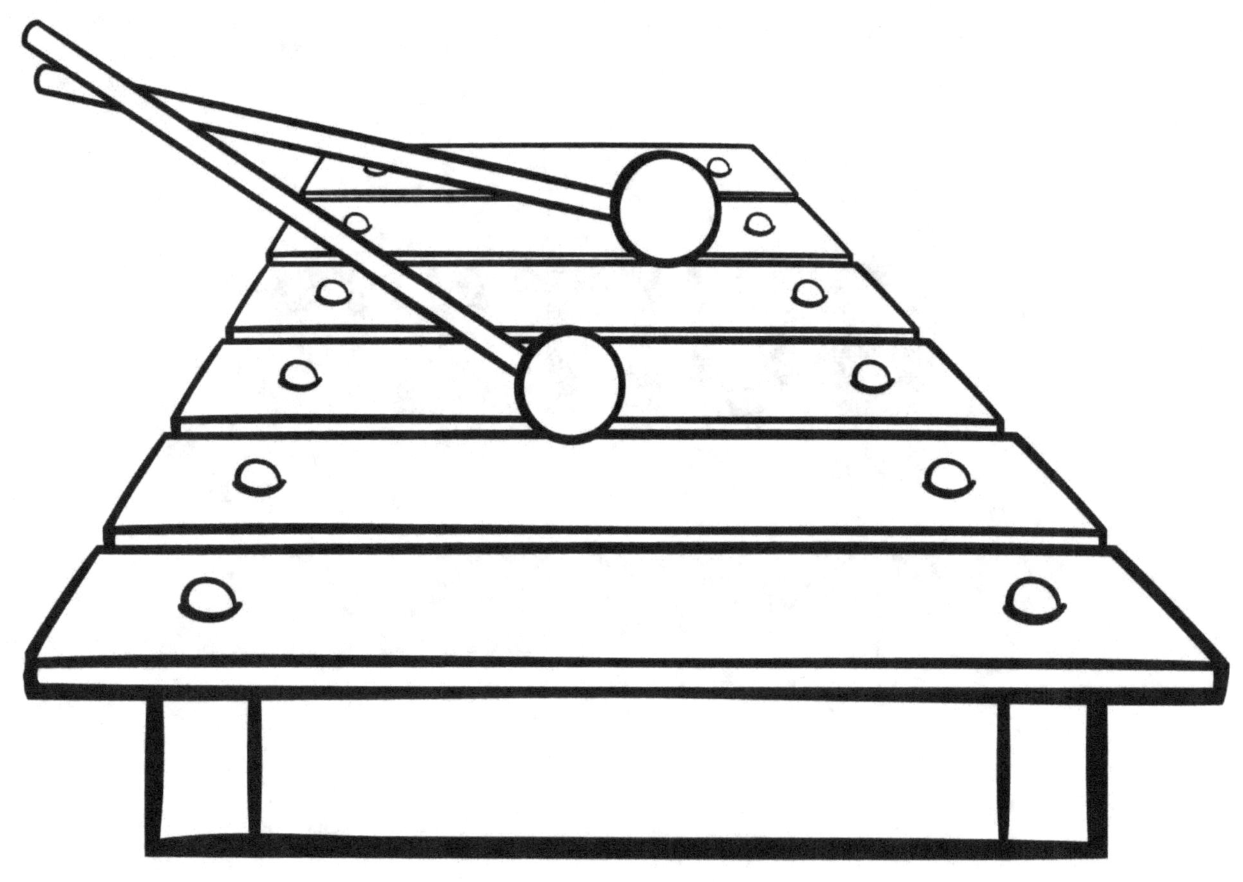

XYLOPHONE

\ˈzī-lə-ˌfōn\

BARN

\\'bärn\\

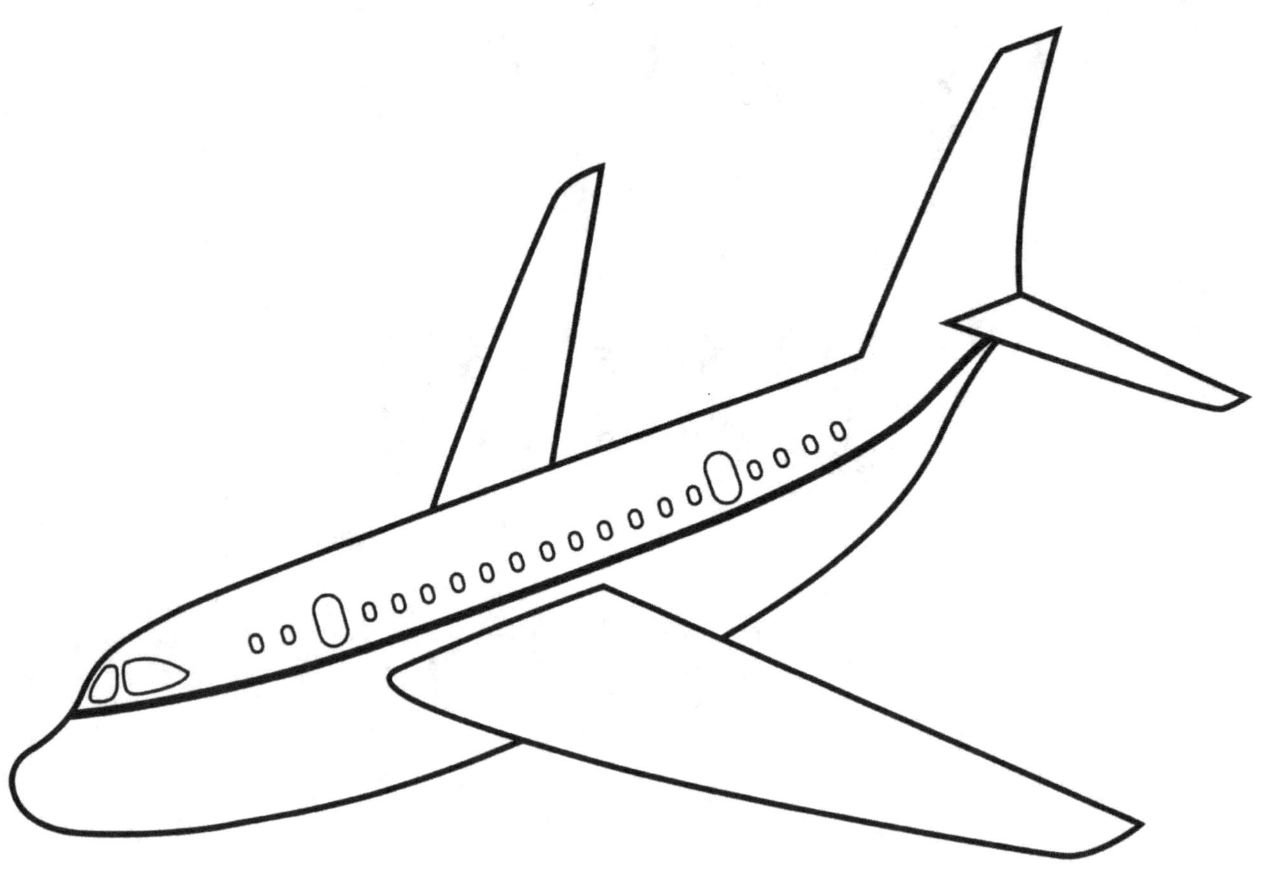

AIRPLANE

\\'er-ˌplān\\